MOVING IN TOGETHER?

Here's some advice to make it last...

A Book of Life
Written By:
Lynn Sanchez

Illustrated By:
Lynn Sanchez &
Farhan Bakri

COPYRIGHT © 2025 BY LYNN SANCHEZ

ALL RIGHTS ARE RESERVED, AND NO PART OF THIS PUBLICATION MAY BE REPRODUCED, DISTRIBUTED, OR TRANSMITTED IN ANY MANNER, WHETHER THROUGH PHOTOCOPYING, RECORDING, OR ANY OTHER ELECTRONIC OR MECHANICAL METHODS, WITHOUT THE EXPLICIT PRIOR WRITTEN PERMISSION OF THE PUBLISHER. THIS RESTRICTION APPLIES TO ANY FORM OR MEANS OF REPRODUCTION OR DISTRIBUTION.

EXCEPTIONS TO THIS RULE INCLUDE BRIEF QUOTATIONS THAT MAY BE INCORPORATED INTO CRITICAL REVIEWS, AS WELL AS CERTAIN OTHER NONCOMMERCIAL USES THAT ARE ALLOWED BY COPYRIGHT LAW. ANY SUCH USAGE MUST ADHERE TO THE SPECIFIED CONDITIONS AND PERMISSIONS OUTLINED BY THE COPYRIGHT HOLDER.

BOOK DESIGN BY HMDPUBLISHING.COM

THIS BOOK IS DEDICATED TO ALL THE DIRTY PEOPLE I HAVE WITNESSED IN MY LIFETIME. IF IT WASN'T FOR YOUR INSPIRATION, THIS BOOK WOULD NOT HAVE BEEN POSSIBLE.

MOM AND DAD, THANK YOU FOR TEACHING ME NOT TO BE GROSS.
I LOVE YOU!

TO MY AWESOME HUSBAND AND OUR AWESOME KIDS AND GRANDKIDS, THANK YOU FOR NOT BEING DISGUSTING.
I LOVE Y'ALL!

I URGE EVERYONE TO PASS THIS BOOK ALONG. TOGETHER WE CAN MAKE THE WORLD A BETTER, CLEANER PLACE.

DISCLAIMER:

THE INFORMATION YOU ARE ABOUT TO READ HAS INTENTIONALLY LEFT INDIVIDUAL NAMES OFF TO PROTECT THEIR PRIVACY AND ANY RETRIBUTION TO THE WRITER. THE EVENTS YOU ARE ABOUT TO READ ARE NOT EXAGGERATED AND HAVE BROKEN MARRIAGES, FAMILIES, DIVIDED CITIES, AND IN EXTREME CASES HAVE TOPPLED GOVERNMENTS.

READER BEWARE. ANY COINCIDENCES OF THESE EVENTS TO YOUR LIFE ARE MERELY A COINCIDENCE AND IN NO WAY, SHAPE, OR FORM, DOES THE WRITER TAKE RESPONSIBILITY FOR POINTING OUT YOUR DISGUSTING HABITS.

COINCIDENCES HAPPEN......

LIFE HAS BEEN GREAT TOGETHER. SO MANY GOOD TIMES. SO MANY CUTE THINGS YOU LOVE ABOUT EACH OTHER. LIFE IS GREAT!

NOW YOU'RE TAKING THE NEXT BIG STEP. IT'S TIME TO SELF-EVALUATE. I'M NOT TELLING YOU TO CHANGE WHO YOU ARE. YOU BE YOU, BECAUSE THAT'S THE PERSON YOUR PARTNER FELL IN LOVE WITH, BUT...THERE'S A DIFFERENCE BETWEEN BEING YOURSELF AND BEING DISGUSTING.

HERE'S A LITTLE ADVICE TO HELP YOU KEEP THE SPARK GOING.

WARNING
SOME IMAGES OR DEPICTIONS MAY BE GRAPHIC AND GROSS TO SOME READERS. TO OTHERS, THE IMAGES MAY LOOK COMPLETELY NORMAL.

LET YOUR PARTNER KNOW OF ANY UNCONTROLLABLE HABITS YOU MAY HAVE.

DON'T LEAVE YOUR NAIL CLIPPINGS LAYING AROUND.

FLUSH THE TOILET AS MANY TIMES AS YOU NEED TO WHEN YOU'RE DONE.

WHEN YOU THROW TOILET PAPER IN THE TRASH CAN, MAKE SURE YOU DON'T ADVERTISE WHAT YOU JUST DID.

COVER YOUR FACE WHEN YOU COUGH OR SNEEZE.

IF YOU CHOSE TO HAVE A BEARD AND/OR MUSTACHE. KEEP THAT SH*T CLEAN.

FOLLOW THESE SIMPLE RULES AND YOU WON'T SCARE OFF YOUR PARTNER
(OR ANYONE ELSE FOR THAT MATTER).
NOW REMEMBER, ALWAYS BE YOURSELF.
JUST DON'T BE DIRTY.

www.ingramcontent.com/pod-product-compliance
Lightning Source LLC
Chambersburg PA
CBHW042259280426
43661CB00098BA/1190